SECRET OF D

MARKETING

BIBLE OF SEARCH ENGINE OPTIMIZATION

VIPUL BAIBHAV

XpressPublishing
An imprint of Notion Press

Old No. 38, New No. 6
McNichols Road, Chetpet
Chennai - 600 031

First Published by Notion Press 2019
Copyright © Vipul Baibhav 2019
All Rights Reserved.

ISBN 978-1-64760-461-5

Do you know that search engines can raise your profit of business twice or thrice if you are on top of the search engines on specific keywords? If you know what your keywords are and want to know the secret of digital marketing then this book is just for you. In this book, I am going to explain to you easy and simple steps which can help you to expand your business and get more sales. This can also make your brand reputation in the market and create brand awareness as well. Without wasting any time let us get started.

You might know that a business is incomplete without any professional website. A business that has a decent website with easy approachable methods can attract more people to your website. More new people coming to your website can rank you as well. It is seen that if people are coming from different channels like facebook search or twitter search to purchase the product then also it can help you with visibility in search engines. Your professional social page gets ranked on specific keywords with little efforts these days. So you need not do any off-page SEO by making huge number of backlinks and getting no benefits at all.

How to make a website of your own?

Simple you can use HTML, Bootstrap, CSS or java scripts to design your website and make responsive and mobile-friendly websites programmatically. However many of us do not have adequate skills about this programming knowledge then you can use some free open source tools like word press, drupal or Wix to create the website. You can design the website according to your own needs and requirements. It is an easy and simple drag and drops in the case of AI as we see in Wix.

I already have a website what next...

Once done then you must use a tool that every search engine optimizer uses to rank his website. This tool is known as a webmaster tool or Google search console. This tool needs to be verified and there are several options to do that you can use simple HTML code for verification as well which I find very easy so you can also use that. Once that is done then you need to make a site map for your website. A site map is a list of all the links of pages that are used on your website. Now you are ready to submit this sitemap. Make sure that you also have a robots.txt file made for your website that guides the robots or bots to come back to your site and fetch your website. This helps in indexing your website on a specific website.

Indexing is an important factor and can easily be tracked using google search console. The benefit of using google search console is that you need not pay anything to purchase this tool. It is absolutely free and need no cost at all.

My website is indexed but I see some errors in Search console

Well, it is time for you to remove all errors that is occurring while indexing your website. It could be javascript that is hindering bots to crawl your page, excessive use of CSS, redirection of website, error page not defined, and many others. Check out the error detail and fix the error as per the given instructions from the search console. Once the error is removed it is time for you now to submit your robots.txt file. You can do this from your old search console as the current version does not provide you an option for submitting the robots.txt file.

Contents

CHAPTER ONE

Do you know that search engines can raise your profit of business twice or thrice if you are on top of the search engines on specific keywords? If you know what your keywords are and want to know the secret of digital marketing then this book is just for you. In this book, I am going to explain to you easy and simple steps which can help you to expand your business and get more sales. This can also make your brand reputation in the market and create brand awareness as well. Without wasting any time let us get started.

You might know that a business is incomplete without any professional website. A business that has a decent website with easy approachable methods can attract more people to your website. More new people coming to your website can rank you as well. It is seen that if people are coming from different channels like facebook search or twitter search to purchase the product then also it can help you with visibility in search engines. Your professional social page gets ranked on specific keywords with little efforts these days. So you need not do any off-page SEO by making huge number of backlinks and getting no benefits at all.

Simple you can use HTML, Bootstrap, CSS or java scripts to design your website and make responsive and mobile-friendly websites programmatically. However many of us do not have adequate skills about this programming knowledge then you can use some free open source tools like word press, drupal or Wix to create the website. You can design the website according to your own needs and requirements. It is an easy and simple drag and drops in the case of AI as we see in Wix.

Once done then you must use a tool that every search engine optimizer uses to rank his website. This tool is known as a webmaster tool or Google search console. This tool needs to be verified and there are several options to do that you can use simple HTML code for verification as well which I find very easy so you can also use that. Once that is done then you need to make a site map for your website. A site map is a list of all the links of pages that are used on your website. Now you are ready to submit this sitemap. Make sure that you also have a robots.txt file made for your website that guides the robots or bots to come back to your site and fetch your website. This helps in indexing your website on a specific website.

Indexing is an important factor and can easily be tracked using google search console. The benefit of using google search console is that you need not pay anything to purchase this tool. It is absolutely free and need no cost at all.

Well, it is time for you to remove all errors that is occurring while indexing your website. It could be javascript that is hindering bots to crawl your page, excessive use of CSS, redirection of website, error page not defined, and many others. Check out the error detail and fix the error as per the given instructions from the search console. Once the error is removed it is time for you now to submit your robots.txt file. You can do this from your old search console as the current version does not provide you an option for submitting the robots.txt file.

www.ingramcontent.com/pod-product-compliance
Lightning Source LLC
Chambersburg PA
CBHW070556070326
40690CB00010BA/2054

www.ingramcontent.com/pod-product-compliance
Lightning Source LLC
Chambersburg PA
CBHW070556070326
40690CB00010BA/2054